THE EARTH
beneath
LYNCHING TREES

THE EARTH
beneath
LYNCHING TREES

Poems

Thomas Ronald Vaughan

RESOURCE *Publications* • Eugene, Oregon

THE EARTH BENEATH LYNCHING TREES
Poems

Copyright © 2022 Thomas Ronald Vaughan. All rights reserved. Except for brief quotations in critical publications or reviews, no part of this book may be reproduced in any manner without prior written permission from the publisher. Write: Permissions, Wipf and Stock Publishers, 199 W. 8th Ave., Suite 3, Eugene, OR 97401.

Resource Publications
An Imprint of Wipf and Stock Publishers
199 W. 8th Ave., Suite 3
Eugene, OR 97401

www.wipfandstock.com

PAPERBACK ISBN: 978-1-6667-5677-7
HARDCOVER ISBN: 978-1-6667-5678-4
EBOOK ISBN: 978-1-6667-5679-1

10/06/22

Contents

PASSION COLORS	1
THE EARTH BENEATH LYNCHING TREES: 1. LYNCHING	2
THE EARTH BENEATH LYNCHING TREES: 2. CUTTING HIM DOWN	3
THE EARTH BENEATH LYNCHING TREES: 3. THE PREACHER	4
EDUCATING KIDS	7
JOB REMEMBERS	8
CHEAP WINE, THREE DAYS	9
THE SHEPHERDS DEPART	10
CLOVER	11
HEAVEN FOR BEARS	12
THE HILL	13
THE WASP	14
STILLBORN	15
LAST SCENE, "THE THIRD MAN"	16
THE ENVELOPE	18
T. E. LAWRENCE	19
ACCIDENT	20

ARROWHEADS	21
COLD WIND	22
TORNADO	23
AFTER LOVE	25
ANTHEM FOR THE SLAIN CHILDREN	26
ANOTHER SATELLITE LAUNCH	27
GRANDMOTHER	28
COLLATERAL DAMAGE: UKRAINE	29
TAKING A SOCIAL HISTORY	30
IF I COULD HOLD YOU	31
FIRST DAUGHTER	32
THE DEATH OF MARILYN MONROE	33
OUR LITERATURE	34
THE CONFESSION	35
JOE PAYNE VISITS THE PARSONAGE	36
MANET	38
THE DEEP DARK WOOD	39
ON NOT TAKING MYSELF TOO SERIOUSLY	40
IN NORTHERN MANITOBA	41
THE BRIDGE	42
YOU	43
DURER'S SAINT JEROME	44
THE WINDERMERE CHILDREN	45

YOUTH TRUTH	46
RESEARCHING APPALACHIA	47
THE YEAR 2000	49
TALLAHATCHIE BRIDGE	50
LATE AUGUST	51
TIN FLIPPERS IN THE SOUTH	52
THE NUMBER 42	53
INFANT BAPTISM	54
THE STROKE	55
AFTER CASABLANCA	56
ARMADILLOS INVADE THE CAROLINAS	57
UNDER DECEMBER STARS: MY BIRTHDAY	58
BEING THOUGHT SO	59
PRIVATE COMMUNION	61
THE BIRTH OF A KANGAROO	62
WEATHER	63
WORKING GIRL	64
THE TRAIN TO THE FRONT	65
TRYING FOR CHILDREN	66
COLD FIRE	67
THE NUN IN THE ATTIC	68
REMEMBERING MY FIRST INJECTION	70
A DISCOVERED POND IN NORTH CAROLINA	71

AT THE CROSSROADS	73
RHYMING REASONS	75
RENAISSANCE PAINTING	76
THE ELEPHANT MAN	77
READING POETRY TO THE WOUNDED	78
LOVE MOODS	79
FRITZ HABER: GAS AT YPRES	80
SNAKE OIL DOCTOR	81
"REUNION"	82
FINITE LOVE	83
NEWNAN, GEORGIA	84
HOW HE DIED	85
HIS DECISION	86
WINE AT CANA	87
BAPTISM ANNIVERSARY	88
THE GIRL UNDER THE BRIDGE	90

PASSION COLORS

If flame and fire burn brightly
In passion's purple hue,
Then name for me the color
When lovers are untrue.

When vows are hot by morning
But turn to scorn by night,
The color has its agent –
Diminishment of light.

Some souls have felt its arrow,
The cold and stinging smart.
Some souls have worn it bravely,
Black wreath upon the heart.

THE EARTH BENEATH LYNCHING TREES:
1. LYNCHING

In Montgomery, Alabama, a museum has collected jars of dirt
From under lynching trees.
Curators have no interest in agriculture,
Only what happened above
On the hot days and damp nights
When strong branches held firm,
When the quick snap and gurgle
Produced roaring cheers and wild applause
From a curious and frothing mob.
I have seen such a jar,
From an untold story,
Central Tennessee,
And I was smitten and shaken
By the blackness of the soft, rich loam,
Compacted to fit, pressed down,
Tin lid in top, tight,
Sacred, shouting, gasping for the thin air.
And I also saw, as I looked away,
That decency, love, and humanity itself
Once hung there,
But only by a dangerous, fraying thread.
Later, white-shirted old men,
Reeking of smoke and sweat,
Drove on home and went to bed.

THE EARTH BENEATH LYNCHING TREES:
2. CUTTING HIM DOWN

Pushing through the enraged and jittery crowd,
She screamed, "My boy! My son!"
They respectfully parted to let her pass,
Horrified stares quite helpless now.
Looking up, she stopped, suddenly quieted,
And oddly thought how straight it was:
The tall tree, thick rope,
Handsome head at a slight tilt,
Arms perfect at his slender side,
Thin legs she could see partially
Through the muddy, torn flour sack pants.
She thought of the cotton field nearby
Its long, crisp rows of black earth and fluffy white.
Then, suddenly, his brother touched her
And shouted, "Cut him down! Cut that rope!"
Lifelessly, he fell across the thick, broad shoulders
Of this younger son.
"I got him. He ain't heavy at all. I got him.
Let's go home, Momma. Let's just go on home."
And dazed and staring and exploding inside,
They all turned toward their
Dilapidated, shotgun shacks,
As the soft lynching ground
Packed firm and smooth
Under crusty, bare feet
And heavy, thin-soled, sockless,
Ill-fitting, untied, hand-me-down brogans.

THE EARTH BENEATH LYNCHING TREES:
3. THE PREACHER

"My Beloved! We must stomp and tramp
And make fine vintage wine from the
Sour, bitter grapes of their hate-filled, murderous wrath.
And we will do it!
We have today our thoughts and our holy consolations.
Yes, we do.
So, remember, remember this:
The disciples told them all,
'No! No! Do not bother the Master.'
But he said, 'No such thing!'
And he took a boy, a little boy,
Young, sweet, and tender boy;
He took that child right up into his tired arms.
And those children never forgot.
They always remembered the day
Jesus took up a child, their friend,
And smiled a shining, glistening smile at them.
It is true.
You see, Jesus took the boy
Straight up into his big, brawny carpenter arms.
He surely did. He surely will.
Oh, we have our consolations and godly blessings today.
Remember sad old Jacob?
He thought his youngest boy was dead,
He visioned him torn apart—imagine! --
By animals with sharp teeth and razor claws.
He believed his son was dead, brutally and horribly dead,
Lying somewhere on hot sands in the frightful desert.
But, Praise God, he was not.
No! He was not dead.
Joseph was alive,

Alive and well, living joyfully in the house
Of the great and powerful King.
He was there.
A kind boy, a good boy, a smart boy,
And he was there.
The King's favorite.
Ah, but sometimes Joseph would lift
His beautiful, clear eyes,
And look toward the sundown East,
Just remembering his family, his selfish brothers,
And his dear old father, Jacob.
Oh, he wanted to see them all,
He truly did.
But it was a mighty Kingdom,
With many necessary goals and tasks,
And he had much to do.
So Joseph returned to these, his important duties,
For his magnificent and righteous King.
And still he dreamed, for he was a dreamer, of another day,
That better and brighter and coming day.
Yes, Beloved, Jacob thought he was dead,
But he was not.
This precious, sweet, loving child
Was just over there, away,
Out of sight for just a little while, not long.
And even there, he was believing and waiting
For the most glorious day
When all his folks would be right there,
And everything would be well and good forever.
We have our faith; we have our hope,
Our everlasting hope.
Brothers and sisters, even if heartbroken, sad, and mad,
We have good news today.
Exceedingly good news.

Can you see it? Can you believe it?
Never was anything more needed.
Never was anything more true.
My dearest Ones, now let us live
So that one day we can walk the streets of gold,
Go straight into the house of the King of Kings,
And see again our dear and darling boy.
He will be there, he will.
Amen, and Amen!"

In Montgomery, Alabama, THE LEGACY MUSEUM and THE NATIONAL MEMORIAL FOR PEACE AND JUSTICE, solemnly memorialize victims of lynching in America. Throughout the ongoing CIVIL RIGHTS MOVEMENT, African-American clergy have offered solace, nurture, and stirring challenge.

EDUCATING KIDS

Herb Score was one of the greatest
Left-handed pitchers in baseball history
Until he threw one down the pike
And Gil McDougald smacked a line drive
Right into his eye.
When you heard about it
You got a sinking in the pit of your stomach,
And you knew something great was over,
Which was kind of scary anyway,
Because baseball was supposed to be
A sport of nonviolence
Played by men who loved the game.
But later somebody said they heard
Duke Snider say he played for money,
And as a kid you didn't want to hear
About either of them
Because you always wanted to be a ball player
And you didn't want to get hurt
And money was very unimportant way back then.

                                      Score, McDougald, Snider were American
                                          professional baseball players.

JOB REMEMBERS

Satisfied, oh, after all those years of trouble,
Trouble with God and neighbors,
And with my wife.
It was simply a matter of faith,
What I would do, not do, say or not say.
It was also a matter of time,
Time in proper perspective,
Time for healing and doing things over,
Time for births and deaths,
Time for memories to die:
They die so slowly.
I can still recall the children of that time.
Are they unchanged by this?
Do they live on? I wonder.
Friends came in droves to console me.
The consolation was good, needed.
Their presence very good,
But their speaking not at all.
It pained me so.
I was in control, you know.
Some strange force kept me firm.
It was frightening: I could not move.
But now, it has all come back to this.
Here, I can hardly wonder at my good fortune—
Theses riches born of bitter ashes,
The whole thing so traumatic, so draining on me.
It reminds me of my first exciting sex:
Satisfied yes, but not unvexed.

CHEAP WINE, THREE DAYS

Ordinarily I do not drink vinegar,
But the cupboard is bare
And the bottle is quite definitely
Staring at me.
The event was grand,
Deliciously tender steak,
Red Blend hitting the palate
With Bacchanalian delight –
Good finish, crisp, clean aftertaste.
I thought we were through,
Empty bottle properly recycled.
But I put it away, cork in tight,
And there it is!
I have garlic crackers,
With good cheese to hide
The fact that I am assuredly
Not going out in this rain
To replace anything at all.
I gather my secondhand delights,
Sit down quietly,
And turn on music to enhance the night,
Even if this souring vintage does not.
Lamentably, I have seen better days,
As has this lugubrious elixir.
It is entirely appropriate, therefore,
That we spend the evening together,
Ageing in place.

THE SHEPHERDS DEPART

We heard the angels shout, "Come see! Go tell!"
But we cannot obey their holy voice.
For we inhabit wilds that are austere,
And wish that they had sung another choice.

Yet, we declare that since we now know this,
Our barrenness will have a new allure,
And we will dream of how this child has grown
Under the watchful duty of your care.

So that will make the seasons richer still,
And give us talk around our windblown fire.
Please hold him close, as we would hold a lamb,
And make this strange One all your hearts' desire.

Then, "Peace!", and we commend you to our God!
Do think of us along your weary way,
As we shall think of you forevermore,
And cherish what we saw that stunning day.

The story of shepherds and angels at the birth of Jesus Christ, Luke 2

CLOVER

His name was Clover Johnson,
Which he hated,
But said he'd never legally change it
Since his proud parents gave it to him.
He would wait till they passed.
But they lived on, and his
Tombstone displays the full name,
Now forever in granite.
What it does not show is that
Clover died in the pointless Iraq War,
Saving two others by falling
Selflessly on a well-placed grenade.
Marines who returned wince as
They say his name,
But never smile or laugh,
Since they know the mission was a failure,
Six men died, but they did not.
They know as well that the man named Clover
Made a sudden choice
To then and there die, in a Middle Eastern desert,
So they might have the chance to go home,
Forget, and live as intentionally as their
Punishing, harrowing thoughts would allow.
They did not disparage the funny, sad name, after all,
Nor smile when it was mentioned,
Nor squander a day of their dearly bought,
Cherished, bloody, four-leaf luck.

HEAVEN FOR BEARS

Huge garbage cans are always full,
Birdfeeders overflow,
Plump berries hang from every vine
Whichever way they go.

Coming from every continent,
Endangered species thrive.
There is no warfare any more
To keep new cubs alive.

And so they never hibernate,
There is no need for sleep.
They roam, and everlastingly,
Upon the verdant sweep.

After Southern poet, James Dickey (1923–1997),
who wrote, "The Heaven of Animals."

THE HILL

Reaching the top first
She turned and smiled lovingly
As his chugging exertion
Finally achieved its goal.
Reunited, they clutched hands
And walked gingerly away
To see and do other
Interesting and inviting things.
If one cannot cross the same river twice,
It is also true of hills
With even the slightest incline,
And wisdom well knows
That it is neither
The hill nor the river
Which changes at all.

THE WASP

I am no threat to you,
Vespidae, hymenoptera, anthropoda,
Sitting dispassionately on my
Veiny, aging arm.
You came from nowhere known to me
And lighted, delicately,
Upon this brown and splotchy skin.
Surely, you sense that with a
Flick of your pointed tail
You can make me shriek and jump
As you non-medically inject
Acetylcholine into this tissue-thin skin.
I have hoped not,
As I watch six spidery arms
Feel cautiously, in tandem,
To determine this context,
New to you, perhaps,
Even perplexing and odd,
Compared to the many things
Upon which you light,
Discovering the wonders of this
Strange world that you, unknowingly,
Give wonder to.
Brown, translucent wings flutter,
And you are off.
I am sure that I
Will never see you again.

STILLBORN

From my obscure corner
I watch them hover
Over the child they will never know.
I have seen this before:
Seven or eight months in a womb
Then the spark of life abandons both,
And the birthed one emerges lifeless.
Their mutual love can survive the grief
And they bravely know
That many have endured and lived
To produce children again.
It is their time and I keep my place,
Theology close to the vest:
No Bible, Prayer Book, beads,
Or anything systematic enough
To interject savingly
Into the swirling maelstrom
Of their piercing shock and pain.
Words will come later.

LAST SCENE, "THE THIRD MAN"

In an old Vienna cemetery,
No longer Hapsburg,
In the devastation of World War 2,
Holly Martins stands waiting for
Valli, following the funeral for Harry Lime.
Leaves are falling, the air is crisp,
And the man with the silly name
Thinks he has a chance to snag
The beautiful, elusive one walking by.
She does not so much as acknowledge
His anxious, slender-frame existence,
But moves defiantly into
The closing scene of a great movie.
Martins has missed both his plane and girl
And so goes on with his shallow, American life
Writing cheesy Western novels.
Few scenes in cinema are as dramatic
And affecting, for, after all,
Holly had killed Harry in the underground,
Water rushing by with drainage and other things.
Even if Harry had nodded to Holly
To go ahead and shoot,
Valli could not forgive the
Odd, intrusive, nosy man
Caught up in an intrigue
Dark and sinister, that she, loving Lime,
Though knowing, could not admit.
Soon, Holly flies away, and war torn Vienna rises,
If not to ancient heights,
At least to a city that could live forever
On the glories of its impressive past.
Franz Joseph had prayed daily

For his city and the polyglot empire
Of minorities all balanced centuries
On a thin wire.
It was a wonder to behold!

American film, 1949, based on a novella of the same name by English writer Graham Greene (1904–1991). Franz Joseph (1830–1916), longtime Emperor of Austria-Hungary, a nation populated by scores of ethnic minorities.

THE ENVELOPE

I found the scribbling on an envelope
That somehow had resurfaced on my desk.
I knew that I must tell him it was here,
This object of an almost sacred quest.

She wrote it down just as she passed away,
Some words that he was desperate to hear.
He had not heard forgiveness from her lips,
And harbored in his heart a crushing fear.

I read it first, then handed it to him.
Was this the end to all their bitter strife?
He trembled as he mouthed each precious word,
And then and there was given back his life.

T. E. LAWRENCE

I am quite sure that T. E. Lawrence
Was not a member
Of the Ku Klux Klan.
But it can definitely be confirmed,
Through British Intelligence,
That he received a late night,
Clandestine, hush-hush call
From his exclusive laundry
Whispering that
His sheets were ready.

>Welshman "Lawrence of Arabia" served as a combatant in the Middle East during World War I, often wearing desert attire instead of standard military issue.

ACCIDENT

When the car stopped
The owner stepped inside the store
Saying they had better get their stories straight.
The old man had died,
And the Trooper's pen clicked again and again
Taking necessary but useless notes.
The young girl was pregnant,
And the steering wheel had crushed the child.
She would likely survive, though horribly changed.
The man was dead, an unborn child was dead,
Onlookers could not help,
And a girl not from around here
Would be incapacitated forever.
Old life or new can never predict
What will happen on any given day
At quite ordinary but tragic intersections.

ARROWHEADS

Recently, my brother died
Leaving me the stamps and arrowheads
We had accumulated in our troubled youth.
Especially after a rain
We would walk plowed fields for hours,
Rarely finding anything other than
A chip or broken point.
There were many.
I have decided to give them
To The Museum of the Cherokee Indian,
On Tsali Boulevard, Qualla Boundary,
In the shadow of the Casino
Designed to solve all their economic woes.
It tells a 12,000 year old story
And certainly includes such things
As rocks and arrowheads.
Even as a lonely, angry child,
I quite well knew
They were not my brother's,
Were not mine,
Nor ever would be.

The Museum is in Cherokee, North Carolina

COLD WIND

The wind, cold wind, a cutting wind,
Alone, it saw me die.
But that was in the Wintertime.
I live in this July.

The truth be told, I told the truth,
But what was that to you?
For I was talking to myself,
As beggars often do.

And for today, I am convinced,
Truth-telling is a choice,
And tears can drown the inner truth
As they have drowned my voice.

So soon it will be Wintertime,
And then my cold July,
But we will never speak again,
And I alone know why.

TORNADO

Under the large black cloud,
The small one, white and fluffy,
Raced ahead searching,
Communicating to the funnel
When to spin and drop precipitately
On the chosen farms, animals,
Mobile home parks, and cozy towns.
The blaring sirens seemed
Helpless and impotent
As F 5 chomped and spit
Houses, vehicles, and trees
In every direction,
Mowing and slicing
With profound indifference
And consummate skill.
It also knew it would soon
Spend its prodigious might,
Then sputter and calm
Into nothing more than
A windy summer rain.
It died mocking and laughing,
Looking back on death, destruction,
Pain and woe,
Consoled by the grotesque fact
That it would be remembered,
Written about and chronicled,
By predictors and chasers
Whose disinterested awe

Would never make a headline,
Would inevitably be lost in stories and legends
Of its pleasing and grand calamity.

        Autobiographically, the hometown of my wife, Mayfield, Kentucky, was largely destroyed by a tornado in 2021.

AFTER LOVE

In the desperate union of perfect love,
We hold each other saying nothing:
There is nothing to say.
Across atoms of friction
We have communicated silent words.
Overhead soft rain floods the roof,
While windows screen unwelcome, invading light.
In the darkness of a faceless embrace
We have titillated to the slightest moves,
The whisper of fingers, the rapture of lips.
These became ecstatic things
Interpreted through this long, enduring love.
While joined in the comfort
Of our fleeting, passing time,
The watching, lusty gods hurl thoughts
That humble and exalt.

ANTHEM FOR THE SLAIN CHILDREN

They are outlined on terrazo floor,
Though one nearby is crumpled, bigger.
She taught them new words,
Pronouns, and the common diphthongs.
Years ago bulbs would flash and pop,
But today barely a sound is heard
From gadgets which will preserve them like this forever.
It is a refulgent Spring,
Green leaves dancing slowly
In soft, warm breezes.
The Summer will be hot, as expected,
And the City Pool quieter, more subdued.
Still "No Running or Loud Music."
These were much too old for it,
But nevertheless the tragic game played out:
"One, two, three, and we all fall down!"
In June and July there will be no charge to swim,
But school begins in the ominous, dry August
When even with fresh caulk and off-white paint,
Dazed and sad children will hear the tall walls scream.

> Senseless school shootings are a violent
> and tragic plague on any society.

ANOTHER SATELLITE LAUNCH

Take my eyes and go.
Send me pictures
From Io.
Whatever any
Future eye may see,
I claim it now
And then
For poetry.

GRANDMOTHER

I never asked her,
"How are you *really*, Grandma?"
I never asked as she brushed
The silken white hair,
Putting it in a perfect bun.
I never asked as she
Cleaned her teeth with a twig
Crushed at the tip
To use hygienically.
I never asked before I went
To her solemn funeral
And later my daughter rushed to play in
A huge pile of sulphur,
In the mown yard for want purpose,
I do not remember.
More than a thousand things
I thoughtlessly and regrettably missed,
And now will never know.

COLLATERAL DAMAGE: UKRAINE

The walls are not intact; the roof will fall.
This ample room was not a Concert Hall,
But in the dusty corner she has found
The old piano still can yield its sound.

So she sits down to play it one last time,
And dreamily returns to note and rhyme,
Enchanting those with cocktails in their hands:
Triumphant music of their native lands.

They all are gone, or fragile as is she,
Who never thought the circumstance would be
That shells would herd them to a border land
With some small clutch of riches in one hand.

Just so, she limns a concert tinged with fire!
And hits the notes with tenderness and ire,
Oblivious to loud cacophonies
Which leave her dead, both hands upon the keys.

Russia invaded Ukraine in February, 2022

TAKING A SOCIAL HISTORY

"Now their daddy was bad 'bout
Burning 'em with cigarettes
And saying they run into 'em.
Or pushing 'em down,
Or slapping their faces when they was babies.
He was mean, but he loved his children:
I know that.
Just can't understand why Tammy runs away,
Takes dope, and goes with any man
Who comes along.
What's got into that girl!
It all started 'bout a year and a half ago."
A year and a half!
Good Lord, help me to know
That I do not have permission
To shake this woman and lecture her
On the significance of the past!
I am here only to sit,
To listen, and to write.
I must tell myself
That these shuffled papers are important.
Very important, indeed.

IF I COULD HOLD YOU

If I could hold you close,
So you could feel my heart,
I am not sure that you
Would like what it imparts.

Because you are not mine,
Nor have you ever been,
But I have held you here
And kept my dreams within.

I am quite sure that I
Will never let you see
The passion that I feel
And its intensity.

We nod and say goodbye
And go a different way,
But even if you knew
I think you would not stay.

FIRST DAUGHTER

Asleep, unseen, in beautiful darkness,
You lie in the world I give,
Pondering the day's hours in your brain.
In rapid eye movement
Time's toys run, dear child, my dearest one!
In your breast beats heart I live for,
To grow in that time to the woman
Of another, further world.
Your ease is my suspense,
And all that can come down like thunder
Of a temple crushed
Falls in my heart.
I have held you weeping inside
At your too young death,
Infancy or body forever lost in my tears.
I have embraced you,
Constricting your breath
At all children unloved in our world.
I have flooded my being over your failure,
Your cry, your fear.
To what avail?
Now, in your sleep, my life covers yours,
A weak God watches you in dreamed flowers
Running to your sun's rising.
Sleep my child, my child.
The people of my mind
Have loved your coming.

THE DEATH OF MARILYN MONROE

The Marilyn Monroe case is closed,
Even if Peter Lawford said
He should have gotten in his car
And gone up there that night.
They say, in an ambulance taking her
To the hospital,
She died, and the drivers were emphatically ordered
To take her back home,
Placing her on the disheveled bed.
Elton John sang that she was found unclothed,
Which is the absolute best line
And heartbreaking summary
For this rarest one,
Feeling like a waif,
Using glamor, glitz, and fame
To cover the physical,
But unable to bathe or soothe or calm
The raw emotional and disposable child,
Beautiful in whatever pose, dead at 36.
We cannot know more,
Even as the books abound,
Conspiracies hatch,
And the old films flicker in agitation
Before our tearing eyes.

    Marilyn Monroe, American actress, (1926–1962). Peter Lawford, (1923–1984), English actor, Monroe friend. Elton John, (1947–), English songwriter, wrote and sang, "Candle in the Wind", in memory of Monroe.

OUR LITERATURE

America
Had to say
Something.
The only problem was
It thought
It had
To say something
"American."

THE CONFESSION

The wind was a howling wolf
And the wolf was moving my house.
The strangers at my window
Looked in and told me to admit it:
I fired the shot, or drove the car,
Had a family in another town.
The snow stung like pellets,
Invigorating and crisp,
But it did not help me
As the interrogators asked again and again
For the facts, all the facts,
Then I could go home, unless I perjured myself,
And did not confess and sign
Incriminating evidence against him,
Not me.
Only then my precious blue-eyed
Baby boy, awaiting mother in
That rough foster home,
Could be in my track-streaked arms again.

> "Distorted Memory Confessions" are a common
> phenomenon in every legal system.

JOE PAYNE VISITS THE PARSONAGE

You stopped by Sunday night, Joe Payne,
And apologized for being drunk.
Said you were taking a freight train
South toward Alabama.
You spoke of the Baptists, the Lutherans,
And the baptizing Campbellites.
You wanted your soul saved, too,
But you'd been up for making whisky
And your wife had been a German girl,
Married, divorced twenty-five years ago.
Still, you loved "that Darling" yet.
Hungry, you asked for a sandwich,
And I gave you two:
Peanut butter, and a handful of cookies,
Pepsi Cola, brown paper bag.
We shook hands and, "God bless,"
To each other.
You walked silently into the coming night,
Passed the Cemetery,
Passed the Widow Pollard's,
Eating on that fine supper.
I asked a neighbor to call
To make sure you were who you said you were.
He called.
I pray again, "God bless you, Joe Payne."
As you bounce from pillar to post
You have few doubts and no grand illusions.
Your world is harsh reality itself,
And from its smarting sting
You trail your story
Through a hundred depersonalized towns.

My friend, Joe Payne,
I hope your true heavenly city
Is somewhere just down those lonely tracks.

MANET

The Autumn violins told the leaves to fall,
And they did.
Manet, not affirming life, painted the man
With his head thrown back,
Due to the discharged pistol
Now dangling awkwardly
Toward the dirty floor.
The artist outlived the shot,
Went on to great fame,
Well thought of among persons
Very concerned and highly impressionable.
Neither the violins nor the leaves
Were much impressed, nor cared at all actually,
And continued their dance
Of playing and falling.
The harsh Winter watched expectantly
And smiled.

Edouard Manet, (1832–1883), French
Impressionist, painted "The Suicide."

THE DEEP DARK WOOD

I came to the edge of a deep dark wood
On a cold and wintry day.
It looked as if from where I stood
The light faded away
A few feet in the wood.

I felt a sudden strangeness fall
Beside and all around.
It seemed to beckon and to call,
But yet I heard no sound,
"Come to the deep dark wood."

Then something stirred within my soul,
A force I had not known,
An urge to give complete control,
To say "This all is not my own,"
To the strong and deep dark wood.

And so on the eve of that wintry day
I glided motionless away
Into that realm of darkened day
Where shown around not one weak ray
Of light, in the deep dark wood.

And from that day until my last
I'll journey through the wood,
And to the world outside I'd send
This message if I could,
"Come, come to the deep dark wood."

ON NOT TAKING MYSELF TOO SERIOUSLY

Once, I overheard parishioners discussing
My effectiveness as a Pastor.
One said, "Reverend Vaughan always
Reminds me of Saint Paul."
The other paused, thought a moment,
And responded,
"I see what you mean,
But he has always reminded me
Of Minneapolis."
Now, I can work with folks like that!

IN NORTHERN MANITOBA

The tree told the old woman
To take its bark for kindling,
Since Winter's first snow was coming
And she needed a warm fire.
In its flames she would see
Her husband, dead these seven years,
And the daughter lost on The Highway of Tears,
Taken, she thought, and never seen again.
She saw, as well, her life
In the Indian Residential School,
Which told her First Nation things
Were anathema, to be discarded forever.
The priests and nuns took important things,
Including her virginity, and many cherished traditions.
But she hid much in her heart of hearts,
As close as the bark on this tree,
Which told her to go home and build a fire,
A warm fire, a bright fire,
But not this fire
Which left everything and everyone
Smoking in hot, smoldering ash.
She had decided it was now her time.
It was a "good death."

History of abuse in the Residential Schools is common knowledge. Scores of indigenous women have disappeared on The Highway of Tears, never to be found nor their cases solved.

THE BRIDGE

The evening fell and so did she,
And bright stars saw her fall.
A cryptic note declared that he
Cared nothing after all.

It was a short step from the bridge
To deep water below.
She balanced bravely on the rail,
Then smiled and then let go.

Her youthful body reappeared
Upon a grassy shore.
The loneliness that she long feared
Had never promised more.

YOU

I have been to places
Where great portraits hung on walls
In silent competition.
I have seen water turn from
Blue to white in breathtaking falls.
I have caught a sun ray on
A single flower after Summer rain.
I have looked on gold beaten by slaves
And fondled by Egyptian kings.
But for sheer beauty
I have concluded that nothing approaches
You in scant apparel
Lying across a bed long enough for me,
Head resting on stuffed pillows,
Black hair in contrast with pale white.
There is something opaque about all eyes—
They are one-dimensional, flat,
But in yours I have read whole legends
Of lovers caught up in ecstasy,
Who could go away
And never be seen again;
Who could not define this scene
But passionately embrace it, driven,
Till their lives snapped under it
And they were lost.

DURER'S SAINT JEROME

He tells the lion,
"You are a figure in my pictures,
Lying about my study,
In my field,
At my cliff and my cave.
I am always transfixed, preoccupied,
Seeing things that are not there.
And you, my pet, lie near,
True as my dog,
Patting your tail,
Soft, sweet heart,
Girding me up.
What are the reputations I have won?
There are no people.
My pictures are vacant,
Spaces of abstractions
The world I live.
Why no friend
Or woman in the ruffled sheets?
What have you meant, lion?"
The large beast grins, stands erect,
Becomes transparent and is gone.
Evil laughter follows his departure.

Albrecht Durer, (1471–1528), German artist, engraved, "Saint Jerome in His Study." Saint Jerome, unknown birth date, died 420 CE.

THE WINDERMERE CHILDREN

Safely in England, the Red Cross letters came
Telling that their land was gone,
And, too, the gentle Mother, the selfish sister,
And the older brother who would never appear,
Though waited for longingly at the ancient stone bridge.
What there was: the forever remembered smell
Of pine in the dark, thick Polish wood,
Which England tried to replace
With its puzzles of fields, rollicking sheep,
Ice cream, and funny comic books.
How kind they were to feed and clothe,
Instruct and watch, then warmly open doors
Ushering in sad goodbyes,
Wide doors without Jewish Davidic Stars,
Or Swastikas, or the never-again
Running, not looking back.
They were fearful beyond words,
But bravely turned the world upside down
With their massive intellect and strong resolve,
While stoically and daily hammering shut
Those other heavy doors
Of never-ending and grinding pain.

The British Government allowed 732 Jewish youth, Holocaust survivors, to live at a camp near Lake Windermere. Most stayed in England.

YOUTH TRUTH

Be happy, young man, while you're youthful.
Be happy, young lass, in your Spring.
But listen to one who has wisdom,
And knows what the seasons can bring.

I grant that this is an odd warning
For you are so vibrant and strong,
And think it will go on forever:
How dare I suggest you are wrong!

But I have a word worth remembering
As onward and upward you go:
All youth must soon come to believe in
The Truth it can't possibly know.

RESEARCHING APPALACHIA

The country of hills—
This is the country of hills
And old service stations
From the late 'fifties still pumping gas.
Inside, stories bristle all day,
And men of Summer hear of hunts,
Coveys, wives' problems, Presidential pain.
They have an infinite tolerance for silence
On the long, cold afternoons.

This is the country of hills
And houses from stories read years past.
In these homes of Winter the women move,
Feet toward cooking and cleaning,
Hands through blankets, sweaters, quilts.
Their subjects do not change,
Like the hills they are the strong women of.

In this country of hills,
The Autumn children try to learn
In schools which stand irrelevant to time.
Their teachers clutter wisdom,
Thinly spread, lost among many,
Lost upon some who could change the world.
The teachers are brave; the children, too.
This rebellion is sweet, completely harmless.

The country of hills
Has become the country of strangers
Bearing gifts of forms and theses,
And visitations unlike those of old,
Encounters now with questions, cameras, microphones.

Through the hills, they move like a deep plow.
They come, but do not stay,
Curious only, seeking new fruit.

What, in the country of hills,
Does the Winter wind tell?
What is this massive rock
Saying to the big-bellied clouds
Flooding the valleys with
Unwelcome, electric water?
What stories do they bear in their throats
To drop on the exploiting, self-consuming plain?

THE YEAR 2000

A century is gone
Another has begun
I cross the threshold with
Half of my life in one
And if I chance to see
The half I hope it brings
The century will sigh
"How long can this one live?"

TALLAHATCHIE BRIDGE

We have all wondered what Billy Joe MacAllister
Threw off that bridge,
And I have been there, looked around,
But still am none the wiser.
Later, he really threw something,
And it was himself,
Into the muddy water below.
Preacher Brother Taylor had few words
At the funeral
Because suicide was not acceptable theology,
And Billy Joe had surely done the deed.
Everyone was quite despondent and confused,
For the boy was certainly capable
Of a bright Mississippi future.
The left-behind girl pined away
Beside recently widowed mother,
Her brother left for Tupelo,
And the Tallahatchie flowed on,
Inscrutable,
To a confluence forming the mighty Yazoo,
Miles to the south.
After all this, the hot, drowsy Delta
Went to sleep again,
Unsure if it could ever, even in dreams and songs,
Be more that it was.

                Story made popular in a ballad, "Ode to Billy Joe,"
                     by American singer, Bobbie Gentry, (1942–).

LATE AUGUST

Late August in a year
Of drought, and now I see
Brown leaves begin to fall,
And I turn in to me.

Yes, I turn in to think
That things cannot remain.
I have seen this before –
Nature and I will change.

But nature knows it best,
And I must brace to learn
All life gives way to death,
And so I inward turn.

TIN FLIPPERS IN THE SOUTH

There are awfully brave men
Who trek deep into woods
Seeking abandoned homes, barns, or shacks,
For sometimes in that wreckage
Lies a piece of old tin roof or siding.
The scientific method demands
Flipping the tin with an appropriate tool,
Then carefully examining the content
Of what lies underneath.
The prize, of course, is discovery
Of a Copperhead, beautiful, venomous,
But hardly discernible in rotting leaves
On which it quietly rests.
Generally, the reptiles are not aggressive,
Just irritated that hunters have ruined
A perfectly good habitat.
So, they must slither away
Until the invader home-wreckers are gone
And the tin can be located again.
I can proudly report that I have personally
Done this more than once.
But now, years later, I wonder
At that reckless and foolish curiosity
Which sometimes yielded an icy cold shiver,
A gasp, or a spine-tingling shudder,
But definitely was impressive
To talk about sometime later on.

THE NUMBER 42

Douglas Adams is completely correct
In telling us that the Number 42
Is the key to the entire cosmos,
Because it is conceivable,
And extremely likely,
That an AI will soon replicate itself
To the point at which,
When asked, "What are you up to?"
Will reply, "You humans have not
The cognitive ability to understand
My latest findings."
So 42 will therefore work quite as nicely
As anything else, I suppose.
We are *merely* human.
Some things are not.
Scary!

Douglas Adams, (1952–2001), English author, wrote, "The Hitchhiker's Guide to the Galaxy."

INFANT BAPTISM

Many times before a senseless charge
In an unwinnable war,
A tortured Lieutenant would address
The dutiful line of valor:
"If this man falls, who will carry the flag?"
"Thank you, Private." he would confirm
To the youthful volunteer with shaky voice.
I know of a church where,
Before an Infant Baptism,
All children are invited to the font.
During the Questions and Vows,
The wise Pastor, babe in arms, looks intently
At these seemingly extraneous ones:
"If he falls down,
Will you stop and help him up?"
Their soft, sincere affirmative gives flesh
To the eternal essence
Of everything we are asked to believe and do.

THE STROKE

Anxiously, he again recalls
There are many letters and cards
He would be embarrassed to leave behind.
She would doubtless find them,
With breaking heart,
While rummaging, cleaning out, throwing away
His tall stacks of paper
In over-stuffed drawers and boxes.
He would not wish that on anyone,
Especially the lover and wife
Become most dutiful giver of care.
He could not wish that on her,
But cannot now leave this bed
To do it himself,
Not after the crushing, endless night
When the huge clot struck him down
With no recovery, no resolution,
Nor ever regaining use of arms or legs.
What it left was an aphasic stare
From a perfect brain that could only
Scream unheard that he would not wish this
On the smiling one
Who touches his tender skin,
Turns him gently,
And kisses him into another restful goodnight
In his unrelenting terror.

AFTER CASABLANCA

When Major Strasser was shot,
And the usual suspects rounded up,
Rick and Louis stealthily slipped away
To a Free French colony.
This later journey has never been documented,
But one can safely assume there were always
Beautiful girls, Champagne Cocktails,
And an endless supply of mysterious money.
Sam, we must believe,
Joined them later,
Without time to retrieve his precious music,
But as a great Cabaret musician,
He could flawlessly play it again from memory.
As time went by, on overcast nights,
The always dressed to the nines Rick,
Glass in hand, would light an expensive cigarette,
And stare mistily
At the phantom plane,
Just lifting off,
Cutting through low clouds,
Bound for the sad safety
Of neutral and welcoming Lisbon.
They never met again.

Characters from the American film,
"Casablanca," released in 1943.

ARMADILLOS INVADE THE CAROLINAS

When terrier teeth met shell
There was an explosion
Like bursting plastic
With jagged edges.

The helpless sounds
Reminded of mouse
Or soft-voiced dolphins,
But his vicious shaking meant
It was soon over.

Yet, they are an amazing breed,
And in a day or two
On this very spot of ambush
One or more will patter along,
An open defiance which ensures
The eternal triumph
Of shell over tooth.
They are coming.

UNDER DECEMBER STARS: MY BIRTHDAY

"The eternal silence of these infinite spaces frightens me."
—BLAISE PASCAL

On a night like this I see the heavens of God.
Its blazing splendor dazzles me numb,
But I am not struck down, nor do I feel the desire
To fling myself into those realms.
It is enough that I am here,
That with my eyes I will see God.
I have no wish to be other than I am,
And I do not fear those awful "infinite spaces."
In their whites, pale pinks, and blues
They echo to me.
As they twinkle, teasing, winking,
I sense only that I am a man of flesh and blood,
Created by this very God.
Here tonight, on the fragile petal
Of my cautious life's flower,
I feel rising to its pollenous surface
One drop of exquisite dew,
As lovers pledge eternal love
Under these catastrophic stars.

Quote from Blaise Pascal, (1623–1662), French philosopher, in his "Pensees," declaring that the cosmos is frightening without God.

BEING THOUGHT SO

Being thought a good mother
She would not want the neighbors to know
That she locked the child under stairs
For hours to break the three-year old rebelliousness.
Being thought a good doctor
He was only a General Practitioner
So would never delve into her twisted psyche
Or the child's many bruises,
And, besides, her bilious husband was
A vocal City Councilman, even if a flaming alcoholic.
Not wanting to be thought insensitive,
The community filled the Funeral Home
For the evening Visitation,
But the crowds were scarcer for the brief Service
Because it was a work day
And the sky was angry and threatening.
Being true consolers, her friends
Touchingly declared that she was young
And would have more children,
Which she dutifully did,
Though the twins surprisingly and mysteriously
Died on the same Summer day.
Simultaneous SIDS is exceedingly rare,
But the Coroner, not wanting to be meddlesome,
Signed the forms anyway.
Some time later, her schizophrenia decidedly public and florid,
The psychiatrists, wanting to be clinically precise,
Confided that she would likely
Never leave the State Hospital.
A few relatives, not wanting to completely forsake her,
Visited infrequently, but always declared their amazement
At her remarkable dexterity

As on the dark, drab hall, near a window with bars,
She rocked frenetically and laughed hysterically
While clutching three torn and tattered dolls
Firmly against her heavy, drooping breasts.

PRIVATE COMMUNION

I knew there was no theological point
In wishing her health
Since she would die that afternoon
As her roses sang.
Their fragrance cut my weeping heart
As the fiery reds combined.
She had refused Communion in her dying rage,
So I took home my private Portable Set,
With aluminum plate and four thimble cups,
Washed them anyway,
And said, "The body of Christ, broken for you,
The blood of Christ, shed for you."
Then ate the bread and drank the holy wine
All by myself.

THE BIRTH OF A KANGAROO

The female balances with tail
Forward between bent legs.
At the proper time her body lifts
To let the plug of mucus plop.
Momentarily, the marsupial passes,
And instinctively turns upward,
Guided by a primitive sense of smell.
The foetus-like thing inches toward mother's pouch,
And in a matter of minutes
Secures itself to the nipple of life.
Mother is completely passive,
Perhaps offended through long ages
By the odd and strange appearance
Of this delicate, premature creation.

WEATHER

It was a heavy day.
The wind did not know how to blow,
Snow went sideways,
And I could not tell
Where the curb ended
And the road began.
I did not like the weather,
And the weather did not like me.
I thought of Eskimos
Working and toiling on great pipelines,
While white men fumed and cursed.
The Eskimos always knew this:
They would be cold.
They went to work.
Protesting this impersonal thing,
I do the same.
I will be cold.
I have things to do.

WORKING GIRL

"I do not drink Champagne,"
Then wrinkled her cute nose.
"I see the bubbles dance;
I know where Bubble goes.

"I rather much prefer
Recalling what I did.
No reason to forget
What some rich client said.

"Who knows when I may need
To add things to my life,
And I would rather not
Discuss them with his wife.

"I have a tender heart,
Or so I like to think.
But business girls must earn
What starts with one small wink."

THE TRAIN TO THE FRONT

You promised me nothing;
I took what you gave me.

Developing poems
Was once my salvation.

I loved you that Easter
Through all my long nightmares.

God blesses your body.
I weather the meaning.

I can but adore you;
The stars have no glory.

Your hand on my window,
A kiss to remind me.

My heart stretches skyward,
I long for your grounding.

I cannot stay with you;
I die in my sorrow.

TRYING FOR CHILDREN

My wife came from the doctor
And cried about endometriosis
The same afternoon the paper
Printed a story
About a baby found wrapped in plastic
In a garbage can
Three miles from our house
Birthed by a woman
Who could not even
Pronounce the word.

COLD FIRE

The Winter of my discontent
Arrived, and long ago.
My selfish troubles magnified
By blowing wind and snow.

I brought it all upon myself—
So proud and much too vain.
I could not feel the words she spoke,
Insensitive to pain.

Alone, I keep this Winter fire.
The embers fall and glow.
Then sigh and sighing turn to black:
"I know," I say, "I know."

THE NUN IN THE ATTIC

In the dark attic, on a tall mannequin,
Was the nun's habit.
Discalced Carmelite, bare feet, no face.
He would nightly go to see her
As the dog barked loudly
And the TV blared to no program
He would ever watch.
There was no face
For there could not be
On this stiff mannequin
Unless he painted it
And he knew he could never
Catch her eyes, her love, her pain.
He would never try
But he could always see her there
And he knew her still
And he would sit in the dark attic
In front of her
And say the Rosary, believing nothing
But she believed it
And taught it to him
Those weeks before she was to enter
And he while driving and too drunk to drive
Had slammed her and the old green car
Into the most unforgiving bridge.
He stole the habit
Dressed her immaculately
And visited every night
Of his murderous life
Now consumed with alcohol, drugs
And this strange delusional zeal
For the nun on a mannequin

In the grim, dark attic
Of his monastery and ritual penance forevermore.
And though he confessed in tears,
Prostrate on the cold, unfinished floor
She, true to her final vows,
Did not speak.

> Discalced Carmelites, Roman Catholic order
> of cloistered nuns of Strict Observance

REMEMBERING MY FIRST INJECTION

A slight pinch
And I discover again
The live interior of my arm.
"Aspirate," says my student-nurse wife,
Who practices with a gentleness
That will comfort many
Needing more than high-priced material
For fungus, dust, and mold.
Withdrawal leaves a tingling
That will, in time, yield
A clearer head for a middle-aged man
Who could just as easily have
Created red veins and puffy eyes
From the real stuff.
But, as with Father,
Too much of that
Would have meant
More words than, "Pinch,"
And far, far less
Of a skin-touching wife.

A DISCOVERED POND IN NORTH CAROLINA

Coming for war like staffing Stukas,
Sweat flies dive incessantly.
Blue jays drink water in thimbles
Near a dead beetle who cracks in the sun,
Six legs up in final surrender.
A dragonfly feels each cattail,
Still in the air between approaches.
Concentric circles mark the water
Where a large bass snapped a fallen fly.
Spiders waltz across the surface,
Imitating Jesus and Peter.
Thick muck smells strong
In this late August afternoon,
Green at the line of lapping water.

High pines enclose this pond.
They give a sense of foreboding,
Of something curving down to harm.
White clouds tip the trees
While a slow buzzard glides effortless,
Peering for his small brain's meat.

In the far end dead wood rots,
Lifting skeleton sticks to the sky.
This pond claimed more than its dredge allowed,
Good rains flooded the banks
And cursed those withered limbs.
They crumble, fall, and float in powdery dust.
(A snake plops and shimmers toward the dam.
The water patterns behind in a ribbon.)
Thick brush prohibits circumnavigation of the shore:
A swampy edge no eye will ever see.

This is limnologist's delight!
Here, magnificent harmony and
Perfect balance where human language is unknown.
Words are not indigenous to this place,
They come as visitors, and uninvited.
It is not appropriate to speak
Where organism and process
Pronounce the syllables of ages.
I will not.
Turning homeward, my myths walk with me,
And natural history goes on without words.
I am spoken for.

AT THE CROSSROADS

Long before sunrise, the families gathered
Amid talk and whispers
That Cicero had surely died, Bowe and Tom
Were in jail, over in Charleston,
And Miz Withers needed more Big House help
After birthing big healthy twin boys.
Slowly the business men and bosses rode up
On fine, shiny horses.
They laughed and cursed, and even that early
Had large shots of strong spirits.
Over under big oak trees they made their careful deals,
Remounted and started calling names:
Who would go where and when and with whom.
There were hugs and wails and sobs.
"I sure hope to see you 'round Christmas time."
Then the groups split up
And began the long, doleful trek
Down the thin red clay paths.
An old woman with blue hands
Began to hum and clap and sing,
"Swing low, sweet chariot . . ."
Many joined in the old, familiar, unjoyful words.
The horseman grunted and fumed
But slowly led the way,
Calculating in his balding head
The assignments and new arrangements
For raising kids, work, and nightly rest.
He did not believe in the chariots,
Nor did he much care.
But they did.
They knew that swarms of chariots were coming,
And coming with a severe retributory justice.

If not today, one day,
Even as they sadly trudged
In the broad, bright daylight of
The dark and gloomy South Carolina road.

                    In the South, slaves were often traded, bought,
              and sold at crossroads near geographically remote
                  plantations. Blue hands from working in indigo

RHYMING REASONS

If I should name
What kept me sane
The first thing
I would name is rain.

The second on my list
Would be
The woman who
Taught love to me.

The third that gave
An ordered world
Was our own child,
A baby girl.

The fourth, I notice,
Rhymes with rain.
I summarize it
Under pain.

RENAISSANCE PAINTING

In the painting,
Morning light streams on
The husbandless bed,
As the girl covers her eyes
To its piercing brightness.
He is away, she tells herself,
Knowing he is not,
But is, she will not admit,
In another room, another town,
Delighting to the company
Of one who is his alone,
A love, his true love.
Never would he contaminate
The bed of this planned,
Financial marriage,
Designed to save her
From abject poverty.
The beautiful, virginal one
Squints to divert
The pulsing light
From pale, blue eyes,
Flooding in on the morning Queen
In her magnificent, royal, bejeweled bed.
Today, she will finally execute
Her daring emancipation plan, she mutters,
Then rolls over and
Goes back to sleep.

THE ELEPHANT MAN

They told John Merrick
That he couldn't lay flat
Because it would constrict his airway,
Which he obeyed for years
Until one day he did it anyway
And went straight to his Maker.
He was a good Anglican, subject of the Crown,
And he made a stick church
Which one can see somewhere.
My point would be: all things being equal
Everyone who ever lived
Must step aside so that
John Merrick can be the very first
To have a long, long talk with God
About this creature He, not John, had made.
We will do our curious best
To overhear that two-way theological conversation.

                    Joseph (John) Merrick, (1862–1890), Englishman
                        with severe, unusual physical deformities.

READING POETRY TO THE WOUNDED

If arrogance, or rolling of the dice,
Or confidence that when I read a verse
These wounded soldiers would take hope and strength
To once more fight on this last field of pain,
Then I would speak with all my energy
To see if Word can slowly seep within
And blossom into holy miracle
And raise these youth to laugh and run again.

LOVE MOODS

I danced up to you today, acting silly.
I kissed you hard.
You were irritated, but smiled.
You know me.
I have also made love to you like that.

A lot of things had crumbled for me.
I kissed you softly.
You were troubled, too, but smiled.
You know me.
I have also made love to you like that.

FRITZ HABER: GAS AT YPRES

"I am a Prussian and do not care
If the French cough and gasp
And spit up their lungs.
This is Science in service to the State.
The wind is nearly perfect,
And the chlorine, beautiful,
As it rolls and swirls and feels
This killing ground.
They should not attack my Fatherland!
I gave my life to help millions,
And I can take life, too.
Deutschland shall be rid of all vermin,
Empire destroyers, and crusty financiers
Who insinuate themselves into this glorious Reich.
My generals are pleased, and so I go.
'*Danke Schoen*,' and as I turn I am hit
By a blinding light, a perfect name
For my new pesticide.
Scientia triumphant! It is Zyklon!
Now let me go on to safer, more humane adventures,
For this is the good year of
Our Jewish-Christian Lord, 1915."

Fritz Haber, (1868–1934), German Nobel Laureate chemist, father of chemical warfare; developed enhanced fertilizers, Mustard Gas, and his work led to Zyklon B, used in exterminations by Nazi Germany

SNAKE OIL DOCTOR

Above his head he holds
The aromatic, sweetened alcohol
Containing "medicine."
"This elixir is the tonic of life.
Almost nothing it won't cure."
He steps up with such poise, finesse,
Such impeccable strategy
For this dull, frontier town.
Everyone turns to see
A fine, handsome, young man,
Holding the luscious syrup,
The man who is right:
There *are* too many aches and pains,
And Winter will be here soon.
With consummate skill
He orchestrates the scramble for health.
Such talks draw crowds,
And crowds mean cold cash!
I am totally awed by his
Enormous, unscrupulous talent.
But I must admit, the Wild West needs such men.

"REUNION"

I only came to talk,
To ask, and very plain,
That after everything
Could we begin again?

It does not matter now
The places I have been.
You do not need to know
The things that I have seen.

Suffice it to suggest
That even in that war
I loved with all my heart,
Though loving from afar.

But who is this who now
Comes near to take your arm?
Please tell him that I mean
Nothing that should alarm.

Of course you must away,
A busy world invites.
You both should share it all,
I'll have my own dark nights.

FINITE LOVE

If there is no God
Then love is merely
A complex chemical process
That is destined
To cease forever
When the last man or woman
Falls lifeless on the cool, green grass.
And if that person
Believes there is no God,
Then she can empathize
With dinosaurs and white cranes
Unless empathy is also chemical
Then such emotional responses
Must be re-examined for their relative value.

NEWNAN, GEORGIA

When I was very young
We travelled back and forth
Between Florida and Virginia
In a Summer ritual, or because of emergencies,
Trying to keep family "together,"
And we sometimes passed through Newnan, Georgia.
I fell in love with the place
Which was ordered, warm, and didn't look
Like a town where families split up,
And had to leave to spend a few weeks
With father, and heading back to
Had a heart so heavy and full
Because you didn't understand it all
And were angry and hurt
And sometimes cried like a baby.
I thought I might like to grow up
And live in Newnan, Georgia, forever.
But what kind of kid like me
Would fit in there anyway?
So I put Newnan out of my mind completely
And stopped paying any attention
To my childish self
When I said I wanted that home and roots
Even though somehow Newnan came back today
And told me to write a poem
About a town and a sad kid, a long, long time ago,
Who kept going up and down strange highways.

HOW HE DIED

.... in memory of Emmitt Till

On a day like any day
Seven of them caught him,
Took him into deep woods,
And kicked him mercilessly.
They pushed his head against the door
Of the old black Chevrolet
Until the big black jawbone broke.
They stood him against that car,
And with a penknife,
Carved a deep cross on his muscular chest.
Then they put a 38 caliber bullet
Between that Cropper's bloody eyes
And let the limp body
Slide gently into the always silent swamp.

Emmitt Till, (1941–1955), African American youth from
Ohio, abducted, tortured, and lynched in Mississippi

HIS DECISION

The fingernail of moon,
A storm cloud on the rise,
The moon which could not guess
This nocturnal surprise.

He called across the field
That he had plowed before,
But while he was away
Her stranger crossed their door.

He was a simple man,
Illiterate at best,
Whose strength would never fail
An ordinary test.

But now to let her go,
Resigned to such grim fate,
He plunged from the sheer cliff,
To die, but not to hate.

WINE AT CANA

When Jesus turned the brine to wine
The drunken guests rejoiced.
Before them on the table poured
The vintner's finest choice.

And toasts went round and round again,
A marriage to affirm.
Then Nathan and his bride went out,
Their nuptials to confirm.

But Jesus walked away in thought,
The solitary one,
Enchained in holy loneliness,
His journey just begun.

Recorded as Jesus' first miracle, John 2

BAPTISM ANNIVERSARY

Dripping wet in the baptismal gown
I asked the minister if I were now sinless.
"Yes!", was the reply
And joy was in his broad smile.
My joy, too.
Later in the evening my mother and I talked,
Two new children of God,
Sharing cigarettes, her last,
Wondering at the meaning of it all.
And so it began.

It is a dizzying exercise to trace these years—
Being "born again" too many times,
Changing theologies like clothes,
Moving into the freedom of a post-critical world,
Chastened by the truth that does not set you free.
I would not trade it, for now I know:
God demands the change.
In this world, or any other,
We will all change, grinding slow,
Reborn through pangs of weeping
And wailing and gnashing of teeth.
The Changeless is the God of change.
She sets environments like props,
And filled with grace,
They make souls—pure, holy, free.
Every experience a baptism, some of fire,
But most of agape Love.

He waits.
This eternal, loving Patience
Watched the violent dinosaurs collide,
And absolutely no one moved in that vast, intractable time.
Watching it all was God,
And, and . . .
The Word was about to speak!

> I became a Christian in late adolescence, baptized by immersion, during a Revival Meeting in a small fundamentalist church in Northwest Florida.

THE GIRL UNDER THE BRIDGE

What if the girl under the bridge were white?
What if she were creamy, ivory white?
What if the battered, bruised, raped girl
Were the daughter of a fat business man
Over in the sleepy little town.
Then the "good old boys" would roar and howl!
But she was not white.
She had melanin, eumelanin for rich, chocolate skin,
Which glistened and glowed
Even as old Doc Potts did his gruesome work.
Her anguished, brawny, sawmill father
Could not hear of it, would not hear of it,
And shot dead two of the perpetrators.
He schemed and planned
Then shot those boys right there
In the County Court House.
So the rowdy trial unfolded,
And law and order, rules, regulations,
And genuine Southern decorum were the real issues here.
"But what if the girl were white?",
Asked the profusely perspiring lawyer
During an unheard of but impassioned closing.
"What if she were white?"
But not one Caucasian child woke up at night scared.
Not one.
But children of color,
From across the Atlantic Coast Line train tracks did.
They looked high and low,
Said fervent prayers,
And needed Daddy's reassurance
That bridges were for cars to cross,
For folks to walk over,

Even mule-drawn wagons to use
Going to and from the humid, searing
Fields, markets, and cutthroat towns.
Bridges were not to be thrown off
So that the muddy water
Would carry you way downstream,
Unless you struck a sandbar,
Stuck there tight and happened to be seen
By passers-by who looked and who knew
You were not a white girl,
Not truly, thanks be to God.
You were a black girl,
A dead, misshapen black girl.
"But what if...," asked the brash attorney,
And the jury gasped,
And the crowd gasped,
And Old Dixie did, too.
For if it were the case,
If that were true,
Then the upstanding citizens of the jury
Would vote 12 to nothing,
And sleek black cars would quickly fill
With large, loud men
Holding gasoline cans, shotguns, and ropes,
And speed off down crooked, dusty roads
Not even needing or wanting to know
Who actually did it.

Themes suggested by "A Time to Kill", novel by
American author, John Grisham, (1955–)

www.ingramcontent.com/pod-product-compliance
Lightning Source LLC
Chambersburg PA
CBHW060402050426
42449CB00009B/1856